Grayslake Area Public Library District

Grayslake, Illinois

1. A fine will be charged on each book which is not returned when it is due.

2. All injuries to books beyond reasonable wear and all losses shall be made good to the satisfaction of the Librarian.

3. Each borrower is held responsible for all books drawn on his card and for all fines accruing on the same.

GREATEST MOVIE MONSTERS™

ALIENS

GREG ROZA

rosen publishing's
**rosen
central**

Thanks to Therese Shea for being there when I needed her most.

Published in 2016 by The Rosen Publishing Group, Inc.
29 East 21st Street, New York, NY 10010

First Edition

Library of Congress Cataloging-in-Publication Data

Roza, Greg.
Aliens/Greg Roza.—1st ed.
     pages cm.—(Greatest movie monsters)
Includes bibliographical references and index.
ISBN 978-1-4994-3541-2 (library bound)—ISBN 978-1-4994-3543-6 (pbk.)—ISBN 978-1-4994-3544-3 (6-pack)
1. Science fiction films—History and criticism. I. Title.
PN1995.9.S26R69 2016
791.43'615—dc23
                                                                    2014048191

Manufactured in the United States of America

CONTENTS

CHAPTER 1

ALIEN MOVIE ORIGINS

Our universe is so vast that many people believe life must exist somewhere outside of Earth. For now, we have aliens on television, in books, and on movie screens. Filmgoers love alien movies. Just like vampires, werewolves, and zombies, aliens have become a favorite icon for sci-fi and horror movie fans. And unlike vampires, werewolves, and zombies—which come with a set of expectations about how they are supposed to behave—aliens don't. They are subject only to the imagination of the screenwriter.

Some of the most frightening films are alien movies. Viewers shiver as bizarre-looking creatures crawl into the light or a clammy arm reaches out to snatch victims. People can't help screaming as an alien bursts forth from an unexpected hiding place. Not every movie alien is evil, of course. However, many of the most popular and enduring alien films feature more brutal beings—the real "monsters" of alien films. Why are they so popular? Perhaps because these aliens prey on our fear of the unknown and help us imagine what we would do when faced with danger.

Yes, alien movies are fun to watch—whether they make us cringe or laugh—but many have deeper significance, too. Far from being merely fantasy, alien movies reflect trends and issues of the era. Government conspiracies, warmongering, climate change, draining natural resources, and distrust of technology are all themes these films help us consider, intentionally or not.

ANCIENT ALIENS?

Before there were movies or even flying craft of any kind on Earth, there were accounts of aliens and their spacecraft, better known as UFOs (unidentified flying objects). Some historians claim UFOs appear in religious texts, including the Bible. In 2 Kings 2:11, the prophet Elijah reports a "chariot of fire" that swoops down and carries him into the heavens. In Ezekiel 1:16, the prophet Ezekiel tells of creatures within spinning wheels in the sky. Some have interpreted these passages as possible proof of ancient aliens and UFOs.

Two great epic poems of ancient India—the *Mahabharata* and the *Ramayana*—describe flying craft called *vimanas*. Although some machines seem more like aircraft we know, others hover or zip diagonally or are described as floating cities. This makes some wonder if such technology was possible back then—or if it came from advanced civilizations from other planets.

This woodcut shows a UFO that multiple people claimed to have seen in the sky over London, England, in 1710.

Mysterious reports of UFOs continued to appear in records across the globe. These reports describe floating disks, soaring fireballs, flashing lights, and metallic shapes. In 1561, a Nuremberg, Germany, newspaper detailed red, blue, and black balls or plates, crosses, and tubes that "battled" each other in the sky. It was even illustrated in the paper.

Many stories of UFOs and aliens throughout the centuries are pure fiction, hallucinations, or celestial events such as eclipses or meteor showers. However, some cases are just hard to explain. Many people believe all these signs of alien visitors could mean life on Earth was guided by alien creatures. Whether you believe in aliens or not, mysterious reports have sparked curiosity and imagination. Writers and artists often use them as starting points for their work.

ALIENS AND AUTHORS

Believe it or not, the first written work to feature aliens comes from the second century CE! Lucian of Samosata was an Assyrian satirist who wrote in Greek. His work *Verae Historiae* (*True Histories*) is a collection of exciting stories, including one about a trip to the moon where the characters witness a war between armies of the moon and sun. Many consider this the first work of science fiction. Other classical works that address aliens include the collection of mostly Middle Eastern and Indian stories *One Thousand and One Nights* and Dante Alighieri's *The Divine Comedy*.

French writer Jules Verne (1828–1905) and English writer Herbert George "H. G." Wells (1866–1946) have both earned the title "father of science fiction." Verne is well known for his fantastic tales of travel and adventure. In 1864, Verne wrote *Journey to the Center of the Earth*, a story filled with exciting adventures, including prehistoric animals and an ancient race of giant people. Verne revisited the themes of adventure, hostile worlds, and first contact with "alien" species in the 1869 novel *Twenty Thousand Leagues Under the Sea*.

It was H. G. Wells who first introduced readers to truly frightening alien invaders. In Wells's *The War of the Worlds* (1897), an alien craft carrying hostile Martians crashes on Earth. The aliens quickly build giant three-legged machines armed with weapons to wipe out life on our planet. As the Martians carry out their evil plan, an invasive Martian plant, known as the "red weed," begins growing near water on Earth. In the end, Earth is saved by a surprisingly tiny defender: germs! The Martian immune system was not strong enough to protect them from Earthly microbes.

The War of the Worlds features several themes that continue to appear in modern alien movies. These include fear of alien invasion, battling superior technology, and ecological threats. The story also addresses the negative impact of imperialism. Wells's original story has been used as the basis for movies, TV shows, comic books, and video games.

Science fiction and horror writers continued using themes established by Verne, Wells, and other pioneers. Starting in

This drawing appeared in a 1906 French edition of The War of the Worlds. *It depicts Martian tripods attacking Earthlings.*

the early 1900s, many writers found an outlet for their work in pulp magazines and paperback books. Named for the low quality, wood-pulp paper used to produce them, pulp fiction magazines featured fantastical stories of adventure, suspense, and mystery. The two magazines *Weird Tales* and *Astounding Science Fiction* specialized in stories of lost worlds, evil forces, sorcery, and, of course, alien creatures.

Although many people have dismissed pulp literature as unimportant, others have recognized the influence pulp stories and writers have had on modern fiction and movies. Some of the pulp writers who have had a hand in shaping our modern view of alien characters include Edgar Rice Burroughs, H. P. Lovecraft, John W. Campbell, Philip K. Dick, and many more. These writers have produced works of fiction that are still being used as inspiration for books, movies, comic books, and games. They've also created memorable space-traveling characters, such as John Carter, Buck Rogers, and Flash Gordon.

MODERN SCIENCE FICTION

Much of the science fiction and horror fiction of the pulp magazine era was far-fetched, unrealistic, and downright bizarre. But that is part of its charm! Undoubtedly, it has had a lasting influence on the development of horror and science fiction to this day. Ray Bradbury admitted his short story collection *The Martian Chronicles* (1950) was heavily influenced by Edgar

H. P. LOVECRAFT (1890–1937)

Writer Howard Phillips Lovecraft is often credited as the most influential horror writer of the pulp era. Lovecraft's stories, most of which first appeared in *Weird Tales*, depict cosmic threats to humankind. Some of his characters are mere people, while others are horrifying alien creatures and powerful ancient gods! Lovecraft's narrators commonly set out on a scientific quest to find the truth. However, most go insane when they discover that alien creatures once ruled our planet— and will again.

HOWARD P. LOVECRAFT
légendes du mythe de Cthulhu

Not only did Lovecraft create some of the weirdest and scariest monsters in the history of fiction, he established a literary universe that other horror writers of his time embraced. Lovecraft's "Cthulhu Mythos" is filled with horrific alien monsters threatening to destroy our world, even though most people have no idea they even exist. The mythos takes its name from one of the central figures. Cthulhu is an enormous

This French edition of H. P. Lovecraft stories features a depiction of Cthulhu.

(continued on the next page)

11

(continued from the previous page)

monster with a scaly body and a head like an octopus! He and many other "Great Old Ones" came to Earth eons ago but are now sleeping, waiting to return and enslave humanity. Talk about some scary aliens!

Many of Lovecraft's friends and acquaintances (including August Derleth, who created the term "Cthulhu Mythos"; Robert Bloch, who wrote *Psycho;* Clark Ashton Smith; Frank Belknap Long; and Fritz Leiber) contributed to the Cthulhu Mythos and helped it grow. To this day, writers and filmmakers are still borrowing from and adding to it, including writers Stephen King, Alan Moore, and Neil Gaiman and filmmakers Stuart Gordon, John Carpenter, and Guillermo del Toro. Lovecraft's characters, themes, and plots have influenced numerous horror and science fiction movies, including many of those mentioned in this resource. The Cthulhu Mythos provides the setting for the popular horror role-playing game "Call of Cthulhu," which was first released in 1981. Lovecraft's fiction has also inspired the makers of video games and TV shows.

Rice Burroughs, while author Stephen King cites H. P. Lovecraft as an admired source of inspiration.

Some modern writers, similar to Verne, continue to write tales of first contact with aliens and deep-space exploration. Carl Sagan's *Contact* (1985) deals with humanity's first communication with an alien species. Other authors, such as Douglas Adams of *The Hitchhiker's Guide to the Galaxy* (1979) fame, introduce friendly aliens, willing to aid humans in their quests. Still others, similar to Wells, write stories about alien violence, invasion, and destruction.

Orson Scott Card's *Ender's Game* (1985) deals with these themes with a surprising twist at the end.

Isaac Asimov, Arthur C. Clarke, and Robert Heinlein are sometimes called the "Big Three" of hard-science fiction. Hard-science fiction attempts to follow the rules of physics, astronomy, and chemistry, even in a fantasy world. This is best demonstrated in Asimov's *Foundation* series, Clarke's *2001: A Space Odyssey* (1968), and Heinlein's *Starship Troopers* (1959), all steeped in the technology and science of the time.

The pulp, science fiction, and horror literature mentioned here are just a few of the inspirations for the development of alien movies. Just as alien books and authors are too numerous to list all of them here, the number of aliens who have appeared in movies are out of this world. However, some alien characters have left an unforgettable mark on our culture and should be recognized for their contribution to alien lore.

In Douglas Adams's **The Hitchhiker's Guide to the Galaxy** *movie (2005),* **Mos Def (left)** *played a rather normal-looking alien, while* **Martin Freeman (right)** *played the hapless Englishman Arthur Dent.*

CHAPTER 2

THE GOLDEN AGE OF ALIEN MOVIES

The earliest movie featuring aliens was made in 1902 when French filmmaker George Méliès produced *A Trip to the Moon*. The silent movie shows the construction of a bullet-shaped spaceship, clearly inspired by Verne's writings. The basic plot is much like Verne's novel *From the Earth to the Moon*, too. The most memorable image shows the spaceship lodged in the moon's eye! Once they reach the moon, the astronauts (who wear top hats instead of helmets) confront aliens who look like people with claw hands. It's easy for the astronauts to defeat the aliens: they explode! Although these first movie aliens aren't scary for modern audiences, they were a smash hit at the time. Méliès's movie makes a statement about colonization and fear of foreigners. These themes are still common in contemporary alien movies.

One of the first movie alien "bad guys" from the early film era of "talkies" is Ming the Merciless, a villainous ruler of the planet Mongo in the 1936 Flash Gordon film series. Although Ming started in a comic strip, his character thrilled moviegoers.

Shown here is the most iconic image from the movie **A Trip to the Moon.** *It shows the bullet-shaped spacecraft lodged in the Man in the Moon's eye.*

He was just the first of many movie villains to hit the silver screen as real-life scientists were making new discoveries about space and our place in it.

ALIENS OF THE 1950S

The United States, as well as most of the world, spent much of the 1930s recovering from the Great Depression. Economies grew once again in the 1940s during World War II. After the war, people had more time and money for movies, and science fiction studios jumped at the chance to create new terrifying movie aliens in the 1950s. During this time, there was a prevailing sense of fear and distrust among countries, and alien movies of the time reflected that.

After the United States dropped atomic bombs on Japan in 1945, ending the war, other countries rushed to build nuclear arsenals. During the 1950s, the United States, Russia (then known as the Soviet Union), and other countries held an uneasy peace commonly called the Cold War. Americans often worried about Russian invasions and nuclear devastation. These themes played a central role in many of the greatest sci-fi and horror blockbusters of the era.

The year 1951 was a good one for alien movies. Three appeared that year: *The Thing from Another World, The Man from Planet X,* and *The Day the Earth Stood Still.* All helped found the alien movie genre and allowed people to escape reality, while also offering a reflection on the fears and problems of the time.

WHO GOES THERE?

In 1938, pulp writer John W. Campbell Jr. published the novella "Who Goes There?" in *Astounding Science Fiction.* It's widely considered one of the most influential science fiction novellas ever written. In 1951, Howard Hawks—famed director, producer, and screenwriter—produced a film based on Campbell's story called

In this scene from **The Thing From Another World,** *scientists examine part of a UFO while a journalist records the event.*

The Thing from Another World. The movie's plot differed from that of the novella. The movie is set at an Arctic scientific research station, where scientists report finding a UFO crash site. The U.S. Air Force sends a crew, along with a reporter, to investigate. Together, the teams melt the ice to reveal a flying saucer. A Geiger counter leads scientists to a figure buried in ice.

The scientists and soldiers bring "the thing," frozen in a giant block of ice, back to the base. Once the ice melts, the alien creature comes to life and escapes. When characters turn up dead, the group sets a trap. The action-packed ending thrilled audiences as Americans outsmarted the alien invader. At the movie's end, a reporter tells the story and concludes with a warning: "Watch the skies, everywhere! Keep looking. Keep watching the skies!" Staying vigilant against foreign invaders was a common goal of the Cold War.

FRIEND OR FOE?

As *The Man from Planet X* begins, an elderly scientist awaits the passing of Planet X on a Scottish island with his daughter, a young scientist, and a reporter. The daughter discovers a probe made from a strong metal not from Earth. The scheming young scientist wants to uncover its formula so he can become rich. Later, the daughter comes upon a spaceship in a moor. After she shows her father, he is soon "zombified" by the ship's ray—he has no control over his will for a time.

The next day, the group returns to the spaceship and meet its pilot: a short alien with a humanlike face with slits for eyes. They help the friendly seeming creature breathe in Earth's atmosphere and bring it back to their headquarters. After the young scientist attacks the creature, it escapes and begins turning people into a zombie army!

The reporter discovers that Planet X is turning to ice, and the aliens on it hoped to colonize Earth. The reporter saves the zombie humans and overcomes the alien, just in time for the army to arrive and destroy its spaceship. Earth is saved. However, the audience is left wondering whether Earth narrowly escaped an invasion of the worst kind or if the alien had become evil because of a human's actions.

The Man from Planet X as well as The Thing from Another World introduced another common theme in many alien movies: the evil, meddling scientist. After the devastation of the atomic bomb was revealed during World War II, a backlash occurred against technology to some degree. There was a concern that advancing science could destroy humanity.

KLAATU BARADA NIKTO!

The Day the Earth Stood Still introduced viewers to a Martian named Klaatu and his giant robot defender, Gort. The pair land in Washington, D.C., and despite declaring his peaceful nature, a soldier shoots Klaatu. In response, Gort destroys U.S. tanks with his laser vision. The wounded Klaatu orders Gort to stop. Klaatu is taken to a hospital, while Gort silently guards their alien ship.

As the movie continues, Klaatu shares a secret phrase with another character: "Klaatu barada nikto." When Klaatu is shot once again, the character speaks the phrase to keep Gort from destroying the planet.

Klaatu's mission is to persuade the leaders and people of Earth to cease violence and learn how to live together peacefully. He says that the universe is growing smaller, and there is no room for a warmongering planet. Earth is saved at the end, but Klaatu

Gort, shown here in a scene from The Day the Earth Stood Still, *remains an iconic movie robot to this day.*

warns, "Your choice is simple: join us and live in peace, or pursue your present course and face obliteration." He says that Gort will be watching.

There was concern the message of peace in the movie was too controversial, given that the Korean War had broken out. Director Robert Wise said, "I always want my films to have a comment to make . . . The whole purpose of [*The Day the Earth Stood Still*] was for Klaatu to deliver that warning at the end." It is another example of an alien storyline exploring people's fears about current issues, in this case the U.S. entanglement in yet another war so soon after World War II.

Harry Bates's story "Farewell to the Master," first printed in 1940, was the basis for this movie. In Bates's tale, the tall robotic defender is called Gnut, there is no famous phrase, and

WHY MARTIANS?

In the golden days of sci-fi and horror movies, many creatures from outer space were called "Martians." This term is still used today, often for comedic effect. But why Martians? After all, scientific endeavors concerning Mars often appear in the news, and we now know a lot about the Red Planet. It seems neither menacing nor as mysterious as it once did.

In 1877, astronomer Giovanni Schiaparelli noted the existence of *canali* (Italian for "channels") on the surface of Mars. This was incorrectly translated as "canals," which implied intelligent construction. In 1898, H. G. Wells' book *The War of the Worlds* told of evil invading Martians. In 1910, astronomer Percival Lowell described how life could exist on Mars in *Mars as the Abode of Life*. These and other fiction and nonfiction publications helped shape public opinion. When these works were written, Mars was thought to be the most likely place in the solar system for life to exist.

Even as science improved and we learned more about Mars, it still remained the setting for science fiction novels. In 1951, Ray Bradbury published *The Martian Chronicles*, a collection of loosely related stories describing Earthlings exploring Mars and its mysterious past. This book has a lot to say about humankind's desire for conquest of alien worlds and the destruction of foreign cultures. Instead of painting Martians as evil or aggressive aliens, they are represented as beautiful, peaceful, and wise.

The mystique of the Martian has faded as Mars becomes more familiar to us. Today, Earth probes circle the Red Planet and crawl along its surface. Men may even walk on Mars in the near future. Scientists now know that if Mars once harbored life, it never developed past the microscopic stage. There are no canals on Mars, and no other structures have yet been discovered.

the story has a very different ending.

THE ALIEN MOVIE CRAZE

The three groundbreaking alien movies of 1951 left moviegoers wanting more. Writers, directors, and screenwriters wasted no time coming up with crazier and more terrifying alien creatures and worlds.

In 1953, Paramount Pictures, producer George Pal, and director Byron Haskin brought H. G. Wells's *War of the Worlds* to movie theaters. This movie contributed several iconic alien invasion scenes to the sci-fi genre. Although the movie's plot strays from Wells's original story, the special effects, presented in brilliant color, made it a contemporary sci-fi masterpiece.

Other important alien movies of this golden era include *Earthlings vs. the Flying Saucers* (1956), in which an alien force and an evil scientist attempt to enslave humanity. *The Day of the Triffids* (1962), based on a 1951 novel by John Wyndham, showed plant invaders attacking Earth after a meteor shower. The movie *Planet of the Vampires* (1965) by Italian director Mario Bava took fans into deep space for a creepy alien ghost story with gory effects. These movies and many others prepared audiences for an explosion of new and more terrifying aliens in the 1970s and 1980s.

The evil plant aliens in The Day of the Triffids *scared the pants off viewers in 1962. Here, a triffid terrorizes Karen, played by the actress Janette Scott.*

23

THE MODERN ALIEN MOVIE

In the mid-1970s, improved special effects techniques led to some of the most inspired and frightening aliens movie fans had seen yet. Film studios realized aliens were box-office magic.

In 1977, director George Lucas's movie *Star Wars* helped make aliens popular among mainstream audiences; it also proved special-effects technology was ready to create more realistic creatures and space scenes. The film became the highest-grossing movie to date. (It was beaten by another alien film—*E.T. the Extraterrestrial*—five years later.) The *Star Wars* movies, which span into the present, are full of good aliens, like Chewbacca and Yoda, as well as menacing aliens, such as Jabba the Hut and Darth Maul.

But some terrifying alien life-forms—truly monsters—would soon emerge on movie screens and set new standards for horror and suspense in the genre. Some would argue the greatest of all is the alien from the 1979 movie *Alien*.

THE ALIEN

The opening shot of director Ridley Scott's movie *Alien* features a cargo ship moving silently through space. Gradually the ship's systems turn on, and soon the ship wakes the crew members from a heavy sleep meant to simplify deep-space travel. They learn they have been woken to investigate a signal from an alien ship on an uninhabited planet. The opening sets the stage for a dark, quiet, and suspenseful horror movie, which some critics have called a haunted house story in space.

When investigating the planet, crew members discover a room full of strange eggs. One of the eggs opens, and a spiderlike creature attacks one of the crew, attaching itself to the man's face. These nasty little alien larvae have come to be called "facehuggers" by fans. As the plot progresses, the crew members struggle to understand what is happening. In time, a baby alien bursts its way out of the man's chest! Fans sometimes call this version of the creature a "chestburster." The baby alien escapes and hides in the ship. Crew members start to disappear. Soon the crew and viewers realize that the adult form of the alien, or xenomorph, is far more dangerous.

Scott and screenwriter Dan O'Bannon based their script in part on Campbell's novella "Who Goes There?" The suspense and uncertainty the characters experience in Campbell's story were perfectly re-created for *Alien*. Many critics have pointed out that Mario Bava's movie *Planet of the Vampires* has a very

The "chestburster" scene, shown here, is one of the most memorable and frightening scenes in horror and science fiction movies.

similar plot, featuring a distress signal from an abandoned alien ship and a threatening and unpredictable alien force.

ALIEN LEGACY

Scott, O'Bannon, and H. R. Giger, who designed the alien, came together to create one of the scariest and most suspenseful horror movies of all time in *Alien*— one that still thrills viewers to this day. Another key player was actress Sigourney Weaver. She portrayed main character Ellen Ripley. Ripley is the first truly strong and independent female character in horror and science fiction cinema, opening the way for similar female roles.

Versions of the alien xenomorph created by Giger have continued to appear in movies since 1979, including three *Alien* sequels. *Aliens* (1986), directed by James Cameron, is

THE MAN BEHIND THE ALIEN

Hans Rudolf Giger (1940–2014), better known as H. R. Giger, was a Swiss painter and sculptor. Giger found numerous outlets for his dark and often unsettling artwork, including album covers and furniture. If you are into horror and science fiction movies, you might already know Giger's most notable work—the xenomorph from the movie *Alien*.

In 1977, Dan O'Bannon gave Ridley Scott a book of paintings by Giger. Several works depicted a strange creature with a very long skull, sharp teeth, and humanlike hands. He also portrayed strange alien ships and worlds. Ridley immediately wanted Giger to design the alien creature and sets for his horror movie. Giger's contribution to the *Alien* movies helped make it a modern horror movie classic.

In 1980, Giger won the Academy Award for Best Achievement in Visual Effects for his work on *Alien*. His frightening imagery has influenced how aliens are presented in movies ever since.

now considered a sci-fi/action classic. It replaces much of the suspense of the original movie with angry soldiers, loud explosions, and a terrifying horde of xenomorphs. The alien creatures have continued to evolve over the years, resulting in even more terrifying thrills for moviegoers. The creatures and settings from *Alien* have appeared in books, graphic novels, and video games as well.

THE GROSSEST ALIEN EVER?

Hardcore horror fans often argue about the greatest horror movies. Many fans believe *The Thing* is the scariest alien movie of all time. Released in 1982, this dark, menacing scarefest has held up over time and is still capable of making viewers squirm with fear and suspense!

The Thing is often regarded as horror director John Carpenter's best work. Much like *The Thing from Another World* and *Alien*, Carpenter's movie is also based on Campbell's story "Who Goes There?" Set in an isolated Antarctic research station, both stories feature a small group of scientists and workers cut off from the rest of the world. They discover an alien craft that had crashed millions of years ago. The characters grow increasingly nervous as they suspect not everyone in the group can be trusted.

The Thing is widely known for its over-the-top horror effects. Special effects expert Rob Bottin created one of the scariest and most memorable aliens of all time in an era before computer-generated special effects. This shape-shifting alien looks and acts like your best friend because it has taken over your friend's body! Bottin created unique and horrifying alien forms for the movie—from a hideous creature made of dog parts to a human head that sprouts spider legs and crawls away.

Carpenter's movie is not just blood and guts. Scenes involving horror and action are broken up by moments of unbearable suspense. Tensions run high as the characters begin to accuse and suspect each other. This heightened suspense explodes when the alien reveals itself at key moments in the plot. The characters know if they all die, the Thing could easily invade the rest of the world.

Having just been discovered, this Thing disguised as a crew member flees from the main character's flamethrower. It doesn't make it very far, but there are other Things to worry about.

Hated by critics and fans when it was released, *The Thing* has gone on to become a horror movie classic, and the Thing itself is a horror movie icon. *The Thing* features several fundamental themes found in many alien horror movies, including an attack from a superior alien enemy and the use of science to better understand alien forces. Viewers will even find a few UFOs in the movie. Carpenter's movie, as well as the original story, has been used as the basis for books, graphic novels, and video games. A prequel to the movie (also called *The Thing*) was released in 2011, which reveals the events leading up to Carpenter's alien movie masterpiece.

ATTACK AT HOME

Alien invasion movies like *The Thing* have never gone out of style. Throughout the 1970s and 1980s, horror and science fiction directors brought some pretty crazy aliens to our home planet.

John Carpenter presented another alien attack on Earth in the 1988 movie *They Live*. The main character, a down-on-his-luck construction worker, discovers special sunglasses that reveal the powerful and wealthy of Los Angeles are skull-faced aliens! Without the glasses, they appear to be normal people. He must convince others to believe him, especially after he finds out the aliens are here to suck Earth's resources dry. Again, Carpenter presents aliens hiding in plain sight. This time, however, Carpenter mixed humor in with science fiction and horror themes.

In 1988, moviegoers witnessed one of the strangest and grossest alien invaders ever to land on Earth. *The Blob* was a remake of the 1958 sci-fi classic by the same name. The Blob is a gooey pink alien—with murderous tendencies—that arrives on Earth when a meteorite crashes just outside a small town. Instead of computer graphics, the movie relies on low-tech effects with surprisingly effective results.

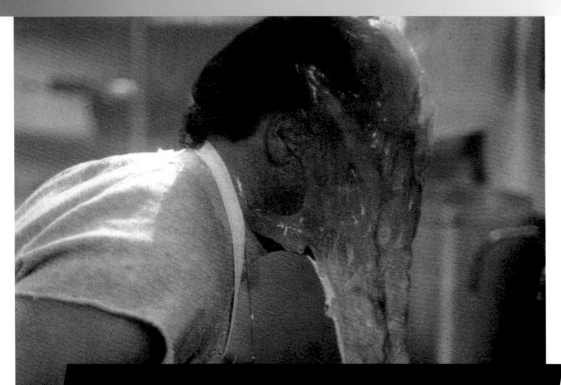

The Blob *terrified and thrilled moviegoers with gooey special effects and gross death scenes.*

Filmmakers began to experiment with different techniques and special effects as computer-generated graphics took hold of the industry. Aliens grew more complex, unique, and scary. Among the movies that benefited from this new technology are *Independence Day*, the 1996 invasion film in which aliens blow up the White House, and *Men in Black*, a 1997 film about a secret organization that oversees aliens on Earth who hide their existence from ordinary humans. Both movies are in the top ten highest-grossing alien films of all time.

THE ALIEN PHENOMENON

Once, aliens themselves were shocking enough in movies. Just the thought of an otherworldly creature was enough to scare and excite people's imaginations. Now, aliens are common subject matter. New takes on aliens are constantly presented to movie audiences to keep them interested.

Aliens have not only remained on the big screen, though. They have been featured on television throughout the decades. Several TV series have provided inspiration for alien movies or have been adapted into movies themselves. Perhaps the most popular of these shows was *The Twilight Zone* (1959–1964), which was revived in 1985 and 2002.

ALIEN TV

Created, hosted, and narrated by writer Rod Serling, *The Twilight Zone* took viewers on half-hour journeys of the bizarre. Each episode—introduced by an infamously creepy intro song—is like a story that might have appeared in pulp magazines, inviting entranced viewers into suspense-filled fantasy worlds in which space travel and alien creatures are the norm. Some argue that this series was so influential that nearly every example of modern science fiction, fantasy, or horror can trace its roots back to it!

The Twilight Zone is at its core an exploration of the human condition and a commentary on how people cope with the fear of the unknown. Rod Serling focused on stories that were strange but also relatable to people. An article in the *Atlantic* reports that he once said, "If you can't believe the unbelievability, then there's something wrong in the writing." Serling drew viewers in by lacing fantasy with issues that consumed U.S. citizens during the early 1960s, including atomic weaponry, government control, and space exploration.

Another series vying for the title of most lasting impact is *Star Trek*, first airing in the 1960s, then begetting movies, and eventually spawning several more series, including *Star Trek: The Next Generation, Star Trek: Deep Space Nine, Star Trek: Voyager,* and *Star Trek: Enterprise*. All feature a multitude of aliens from different worlds as the main characters roam galaxies seeking new life and new civilizations. While this backdrop is fantasy and adventure, the creator, Gene Roddenberry, intended for each storyline also to make statements about cultural issues, including war, racism, sexism, human rights, and technology.

Another successful television series, *The X-Files*, ran from 1993 to 2002. It followed the cases of two FBI agents and their

In the first season of Star Trek, Gorn the alien reptile threatens to kill Captain James T. Kirk. Gorn made future appearances in Star Trek comics, books, and video games.

mission to uncover the truth about UFOs and aliens. A theme throughout the series, and a recurring theme in much alien fiction, is that there is a government conspiracy to hide the truth about extraterrestrial life from the public. The show drew upon UFO and alien accounts passed down over the years, and it later spawned the movies *The X-Files* (1998) and *The X-Files: I Want to Believe* (2008) and an anticipated 2016 reboot.

ALIEN INSPIRATION

Inspiration for modern alien movies comes from many places, but in recent years, many are remakes of past films. *Invasion of the Body Snatchers* (1956), a movie in which aliens take over the bodies of humans, has been adapted several times, most recently in 2007 as *The Invasion. The Day the Earth Stood Still* was remade in 2008. Neither were box-office hits. Having the technology to remake classic movies and add superior special effects does not always mean success in the theaters. However, 2005's *War of the Worlds*, starring Tom Cruise and some incredible special effects, earned more than $234 million!

Some alien movies are an homage to the genre. In 2013, director Guillermo del Toro—an enthusiastic pulp magazine reader—brought his movie *Pacific Rim* to audiences. He introduces two alien monsters in the form of a reptile and a crablike monster that emerge from beneath Earth's crust to prepare Earth for colonization. The box office smash is guaranteeing a sequel.

Sometimes the movies themselves inspire more media. *Pitch Black*, a 2000 film, followed the exploits of a dangerous criminal, Richard Riddick, who crash lands with others on a seemingly empty desert planet. However, a swarm of alien predators is among them, and they must find out how to escape. The movie, a cult hit, spawned sequels, video games, and novels.

Beloved science fiction stories are still being brought to life, too, such as Robert Heinlein's *Starship Troopers*. While not strictly

ALIEN INVASION!...JUST KIDDING

On October 30, 1938, Americans across the country panicked as they listened to radio reports of Martians crash landing on Earth and attacking people. Evening dance music was interrupted by a report of explosions detected on Mars. Not long after, another report interrupted regular programming to tell listeners of a fiery explosion in Princeton, New Jersey. At this point, many Americans fled their homes and ran for safety!

While many Americans thought an alien invasion had begun, it was really just a radio adaptation of H. G. Wells's *War of the Worlds*, created and performed by Orson Welles. Welles planned the Halloween scare to help get more people to listen to his dramatic radio broadcasts. However, Welles had no idea his pretend radio show would cause a real panic!

Although the show included announcements that the show was based on a novel, many people didn't listen long enough to hear them. Many people tuned in to hear a reporter describing a hideous alien emerging from a UFO and incinerating the countryside. All over the nation, people called their radio stations, police departments, and newspapers. Hysterical people who thought the world was ending fled in their cars for somewhere safe.

Once people realized the report was not real, many were angry. Some people even tried to sue Welles. Despite the widespread panic, the American public learned a valuable lesson: You can't always believe everything you hear on the news!

following the book's original plot or themes, the 1997 movie's protagonists go to war with an arachnid-like alien species, just as in the original story. Misunderstood by many viewers, this movie is considered by many fans to be a satirical look at both military and fascist societies.

COMIC BOOKS AND VIDEO GAMES

Comic books as well as video games welcome the wildest re-imaginings of aliens and alien worlds. Over the years, movies have both inspired comics and been inspired by them.

Dark Horse Comics adapted the *Alien* universe to comic books, beginning in 1988, continuing the storyline of *Alien* and adapting to changes according to the films. The company released the stories in mini-series, single comics, and short stories. *Aliens vs. Predator* was a comic book before it became the 2004 film *Alien vs. Predator*, pitting two of the scariest aliens against each other.

The *Men in Black* movies are based on a comic book series. Marvel Comics now owns and publishes this series. The Marvel Comics universe also includes numerous other aliens that have recently crossed over into the movie world, including those in *Guardians of the Galaxy, Thor,* and *The Avengers.*

DC Comics hosts perhaps the most famous alien of all—Superman! Superman, from the planet Krypton but raised on Earth, battles villains, some human and some not, to protect his adopted home planet. There have been many Superman movies over the years.

Aliens have played an important role in video games as well. Even the earliest videos games—such as *Asteroids, Space*

Will Smith's character in Men in Black experiences "culture shock" when he learns the truth of aliens living on Earth.

Invaders, and *Missile Command*—featured UFOs and alien invasions. Today, some of the most popular alien video games include *Doom, Half-Life, Starcraft, Halo,* and many games based on the *Alien* movie franchise.

ALIEN ENCOUNTERS

Science fiction conventions around the country and around the world are ideal places to meet other fans of alien media. There

MARS ATTACKS!

Mars Attacks! is a sci-fi/horror trading card set from 1962. The fifty-five original cards depict a Martian invasion led by humanoid creatures with large eyes, huge exposed brains, and high-tech space gear. The first card in the set shows a Martian army boarding UFOs, preparing for the trip to Earth. As the story unfolds, the cards show Martians attacking people in horrible and bloody ways. The final cards tell how Earth's forces rally to defeat the hideous aliens and destroy Mars.

These trading cards were a big hit with kids, but the cartoon gore and violence outraged parents. The company halted production while parents threw many of the cards in the garbage. Today, the original cards are highly collectible. In 2008, a single card from the set sold for $3,600. No collectors have ever found an unopened pack, which sold for five cents; if one is ever discovered, it could sell for $4,000 or more. The cards have been reprinted over the years. In 1994, forty-five new cards were created for the set, and a series of comic books was released as well.

In 1996, director Tim Burton released a comedy/sci-fi movie based on the trading cards, appropriately titled Mars Attacks! The movie features Jack Nicholson (in two roles), Glenn Close, Danny DiVito, Michael J. Fox, and Sarah Jessica Parker. It also features the big-brained, evil Martians—who only say "ACK ACK!" The movie remains a cult classic to this day.

are numerous annual Comic-Cons, which are conventions that showcase science fiction and fantasy comics, artists, television and movie directors, writers, and actors. Comic-Con fans are known for their enthusiasm and often dress as their favorite characters. In San Diego, California, alone—host of the largest Comic-Con—attendance for the weekend event has surpassed 130,000 in recent years.

For those interested in contacting others more interested in the possibility that aliens truly do exist, each year Roswell, New Mexico—home to the International UFO Museum—holds a UFO Festival. People wear alien costumes and take part in activities such as parades and contests. Scientists, authors, and other guest speakers give talks about the possibility of alien life.

Undoubtedly, people will remain fascinated with the idea of aliens. As Arthur C. Clarke of *2001: A Space Odyssey* fame once said, "Two possibilities exist: Either we are alone in the universe or we are not. Both are equally terrifying." The possibility that life is out there tests the boundaries of our imagination: What would it look like? How would it act? How would our lives change after first contact? These questions and more will continue to be explored through movies and other media in years to come.

FILMOGRAPHY

A Trip to the Moon (1902)
Directed by Georges Méliès.
Starring Georges Méliès and Jules-Eugène Legris.

THX 1138 (1970)
Directed by George Lucas.
Starring Robert Duvall, Donald Pleasance, and Maggie McOmie.

The Man from Planet X (1951)
Directed by Edgar G. Ulmer.
Starring Robert Clarke and Margaret Field.

The Thing from Another World (1951)
Directed by Christian Nyby, Howard Hawks.
Starring Kenneth Tobey and Margaret Sheridan.

The Day the Earth Stood Still (1951)
Directed by Robert Wise.
Starring Michael Rennie and Patricia Neal.

Alien (1979)
Directed by Ridley Scott.
Starring Sigourney Weaver and Tom Skerritt.

The Thing (1982)
Directed by John Carpenter.
Starring Kurt Russell and Wilford Brimley.

War of the Worlds (2005)
Directed by Steven Spielberg.
Starring Tom Cruise and Dakota Fanning.

GLOSSARY

CHRONICLES A record of related events told in a factual way.

EPIC A long poem, usually about the fantastic actions of a hero.

FRANCHISE A collection of media (such as movies) based on or licensed from an original concept or work of art.

GEIGER COUNTER A device that measures radioactivity.

GENRE A category of art characterized by similarities in style, form, or subject matter.

GROSS Total profit.

HOMAGE An expression of admiration for the work of another person.

IMPERIALISM The actions of one nation controlling another, usually smaller or weaker, nation.

MOOR A large area of open land that is not good for farming.

MYTHOS Mythology. In literature, a fictional universe that multiple authors contribute to.

NOVELLA A work of writing that is longer than a short story but shorter than a novel.

OBLITERATION Complete destruction.

SATIRIST A writer of satire, which is a literary work that is often comical and emphasizes human weaknesses.

SCREENWRITER Someone who writes a screenplay, or the script used when making a movie.

SUSPENSE A sense of excitement or doubt that comes from not knowing how something will end.

TALKIE A term for the first motion pictures with sound and dialogue.

FOR MORE INFORMATION

International UFO Museum and Research Center
114 North Main Street
Roswell, NM 88203
(800) 822-3545
Website: http://www.roswellufomuseum.com
This museum is dedicated to UFO sightings and information, including the mysterious wreckage found in Roswell in 1947. Check out the videos on its website.

Montreal Science Fiction and Fantasy Association (MonSFFA)
c/o Sylvain St-Pierre
4456 Boulevard Sainte-Rose
Laval, QC H7R 1Y6
Canada
Website: http://www.monsffa.com/monsffa.html
MonSFFA is a Montreal-based organization formed to promote activities that engage science fiction and fantasy fans. Its wide-ranging interests include literature, movies, television, comics, gaming, art, animation, scale-model building, costuming, and collecting.

WEBSITES

Because of the changing nature of Internet links, Rosen Publishing has developed an online list of websites related to the subject of this book. This site is updated regularly. Please use this link to access the list:

http://www.rosenlinks.com/GMM/Alien

FOR FURTHER READING

Bankston, John. *Ray Bradbury.* New York, NY: Chelsea House, 2011.

Brode, Douglas, and Carol Serling. *Rod Serling and The Twilight Zone: The 50th Anniversary Tribute.* Fort Lee, NJ: Barricade, 2009.

Coppens, Philip. *Ancient Aliens: Close Encounters with Human History.* New York, NY: Rosen Publishing, 2014.

DeMichael, Tom. *Modern Sci-fi Films FAQ: All That's Left to Know About Time Travel, Alien, Robot, and Out-of-This-World Movies Since 1970.* Milwaukee, WI: Applause Theatre & Cinema Books, 2014.

Goldfarb, Ian M., and Janna Silverstein. *Searching for Close Encounters with Aliens.* New York, NY: Rosen Central, 2012.

Lovecraft, H. P. *H.P. Lovecraft Goes to the Movies: The Classic Stories That Inspired the Classic Horror Films.* New York, NY: Fall River Press, 2011.

Luokkala, Barry B. *Exploring Science Through Science Fiction.* New York. NY: Springer, 2013.

McCall, Gerrie, and Chris McNab. *Movie Monsters.* New York, NY: Gareth Stevens Publishing, 2011.

Miller, Davis Worth, et al. *H. G. Wells's The War of the Worlds: A Graphic Novel.* North Mankato, MN: Stone Arch Books, 2014.

Shea, Therese. *Investigating UFOs and Aliens.* New York, NY: Britannica Educational Publishing, in association with Rosen Educational Services, 2015.

Twentieth Century Fox Film Corporation. *Alien the Archive: The Ultimate Guide to Classic Movies.* London, England: Titan Books, 2014.

Warren, Bill. *Keep Watching the Skies! American Science Fiction Movies of the Fifties.* Jefferson, NC: McFarland & Co., 2010.

Wolny, Philip. *Isaac Asimov.* New York, NY: Rosen Publishing, 2015.

BIBLIOGRAPHY

Barsanti, Chris. *The Science Fiction Movie Guide: The Universe of Film from Alien to Zardoz*. Canton, MI: Visible Ink Press, 2014.

Biography.com. "Herbert George Wells." A&E Television Networks. Retrieved December 2, 2014 (http://www.biography.com/people/hg-wells-39224#early-life).

Biography.com. "Jules Verne." A&E Television Networks. Retrieved December 2, 2014 (http://www.biography.com/people/jules-verne-9517579#synopsis).

Clarkefoundation.org. "Sir Arthur's Quotations." The Arthur C. Clarke Foundation. Retrieved December 2, 2014 (http://www.clarkefoundation.org/sample-page/sir-arthurs-quotations).

DeMichael, Tom. *Modern Sci-fi Films FAQ: All That's Left to Know About Time Travel, Alien, Robot, and Out-of-This-World Movies Since 1970*. Milwaukee, WI: Applause Theatre & Cinema Books, 2014.

Fredericks, S. C. "Lucian's *True History* as SF." DePauw University. March 1976. Retrieved December 2, 2014 (http://www.depauw.edu/sfs/backissues/8/fredericks8art.htm).

Glew, Kevin. "1962 Topps Mars Attacks Set – Martians Still Have Hobby Appeal." PSAcard.com. August 11, 2009. Retrieved December 2, 2014 (http://www.psacard.com/Articles/ArticleView/5822/1962-topps-mars-attacks-set-martians-still-have-hobby-appeal).

HRGigermuseum.com. "Biography." Retrieved December 2, 2014 (http://www.hrgigermuseum.com/index2.php?option=bio&act=l&pg=11&lang=en).

IMDB.com. *Internet Movie Database*. Credits for all movies. Retrieved December 2, 2014 (http://www.imdb.com).

LaFrance, Adrienne. "How the *Twilight* Zone Predicted Our Paranoid Present." *Atlantic*, December 13, 2013. Retrieved December 2, 2014 (http://www.theatlantic.com/entertainment/archive/2013/12/how-em-the-twilight-zone-em-predicted-our-paranoid-present/282700).

Marcek, J. C. "Building the Perfect Star Beast: The Antecedents of Alien." PopMatters.com. November 20, 2012. Retrieved December 2, 2014 (http://www.popmatters.com/column/165516-building-the-perfect-star-beast-the-antecedents-of-alien).

Rosenberg, Jennifer. "War of the Worlds Radio Broadcast Causes Panic." About Education. Retrieved December 2, 2014 (http://history1900s.about.com/od/1930s/a/warofworlds.htm).

Schumer, Arlen. "The Twilight Zone Forever." The Paley Center for Media. Retrieved December 2, 2014 (http://www.paleycenter.org/the-twilight-zone-forever).

TCM.com. *Turner Movie Classics*. Retrieved December 2, 2014 (http://www.tcm.com).

Theofficialjohncarpenter.com. "Production Notes." Retrieved December 2, 2014 (http://www.theofficialjohncarpenter.com/pages/themovies/th/thpronotes.html).

Twentieth Century Fox Film Corporation. *Alien the Archive: The Ultimate Guide to Classic Movies*. London, England: Titan Books, 2014.

UFO Evidence. Retrieved December 8, 2014 (http://www.ufoevidence.org).

INDEX

ABOUT THE AUTHOR

Greg Roza is a lifelong fan of the horror and science fiction genres. He started reading H. P. Lovecraft and Stephen King in middle school, and he's loved zombie and alien movies from about the same time. His favorite alien movies include *Alien, The Thing, Event Horizon,* and *Pitch Black.* Roza has been creating educational materials for children for fifteen years. He lives in Hamburg, New York, with his wife and three children.

PHOTO CREDITS